Collins

Livemocha ACTIVE GERMAN

HarperCollins Publishers
77–85 Fulham Palace Road
London W6 8JB
Great Britain

www.collinslanguage.com

First edition 2011

Reprint 10 9 8 7 6 5 4 3 2 1
© HarperCollins Publishers 2011

ISBN (UK edition) 978-0-00-737354-3
ISBN (export edition) 978-0-00-741978-4
ISBN (US edition) 978-0-87779-556-8

Collins® is a registered trademark of HarperCollins Publishers Limited

A catalogue record for this book is available from the British Library

Typeset by Macmillan Publishing Services

Audio material recorded and produced by Networks SRL, Milan

Printed and Bound in China by Leo Paper Products Ltd.
Series Editor: Rob Scriven

INTRODUCTION

Welcome to your Livemocha Active German experience! This new course goes above and beyond what a traditional book-based course can offer. With its focus on online learning, Active German provides the opportunity not just to study but to experience the language for yourself by interacting with native speakers online.

Why go online?

Studying a language online allows you to learn in a more natural atmosphere – watching people interact in a **video** is far more lifelike than listening to conversations on a CD. After watching a video dialog, you will be walked through an explanation of some of the **grammar** and **vocabulary** items that were introduced in the new dialog. Then, by completing a variety of **interactive quizzes**, the system will instantly be able to tell you how well you are doing. You can then **talk online** with native German speakers to practice what you've learned.

Who else is online?

Livemocha boasts over 7 million members and is growing every day. These members are online for the same reason as you – to learn and experience a new language. Native German-speaking members will be happy to read through your written and spoken submissions and to give you feedback on how you're doing. You can also connect with people who want to chat in any given language – interaction on an informal, nonacademic basis is an ideal way for you to perfect your language skills.

What do the books do?

The four accompanying books are designed to complement the online course – the dialogs for all of the videos that you can watch online are available here for you to study whenever you don't have access to the Internet. You will also find all of the Grammar and Vocabulary sections explained in the books, plus the culture notes to teach you a little about Germany.

LEVEL 1

This book is the first of four. It corresponds with Level 1 of the online course.

Level 1 is ideal for students who are newcomers to the language or for those who need to start from the basics.

What you will learn
- How to talk about yourself and where you are from
- How to use articles, ask questions and form negative and plural statements
- How to talk about possession
- How to form the present tense
- Vocabulary for numbers, the alphabet, jobs, the weather, rooms of the house, furniture and household objects, telling the time, days of the week and months of the year

 Every time you see this coffee cup symbol in these books, it indicates the presence of a pathway – a guide to exactly where you can find that particular piece of content online. Log on at www.livemocha.com and follow the path to find the online version of what you are studying in the book.

Video Dialog

A warm welcome for Matthias as he gets to know his new colleagues a little better.

 Active German: Level 1 > Unit 2 > Lesson 1 > Video dialog

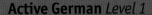

1

Lesson 1: Arrival – At the train station 1

- » How to introduce yourself: *Ich heiße...*
- » How to greet someone and say how you are: *Guten Tag, wie geht es Ihnen?*
- » How to form verbs: *Ich heiße, er heißt ...*, *Ich komme, er kommt.*
- » Vocabulary for titles: *Herr/Frau.*
- » Vocabulary for nationalities.

Lesson 2: Arrival – At the train station 2

- » How to give information about yourself.
- » How to spell out words in German.
- » How verbs work: *Ich trinke.*
- » How to form questions: *Was trinken Sie?*

☼ Collins | **Livemocha™**

UNIT 1 › LESSON 1

Arrival – At the train station 1

Culture note ⓘ

German is not only spoken in Germany. Today it has over 100 million speakers and it is the official language in Germany and Austria. It is one of the official languages of Switzerland and is also used in parts of Belgium, Luxembourg, Liechtenstein, and northern Italy. Over 80 million people speak German as a foreign language.

Video Dialog

Mr. Buschel is at the train station, waiting to collect Matthias.
When Matthias arrives they introduce themselves.

 Watch the video dialog online at
Active German: Level 1 > Unit 1 > Lesson 1 > Video dialog

Herr Buschel:	*Herr Meisinger?*
Matthias:	*Ja.*
Herr Buschel:	*Guten Tag. Ich heiße Philip Buschel. Ich bin Ihr Kollege. Willkommen in Pulheim bei Köln und willkommen bei Waterfront & Co.*
Matthias:	*Guten Tag. Matthias Meisinger.*
Herr Buschel:	*Wie geht es Ihnen?*
Matthias:	*Danke gut. Und Ihnen?*
Herr Buschel:	*Gut.*
Matthias:	*Woher kommen Sie, Herr Buschel?*
Herr Buschel:	*Ich komme aus Österreich. Und Sie?*
Matthias:	*Ich komme aus München.*

....

Mr. Buschel:	Mr. Meisinger?
Matthias:	Yes.
Mr. Buschel:	Hello, my name is Philip Buschel. I'm your colleague. Welcome to Pulheim in Cologne and welcome to Waterfront & Co.
Matthias:	Hello. Matthias Meisinger.

Mr. Buschel:	How are you?
Matthias:	Good, thank you. And you?
Mr. Buschel:	Good.
Matthias:	Where do you come from, Mr. Buschel?
Mr. Buschel:	I come from Austria. And you?
Matthias:	I come from Munich.

Grammar

In this section we go over some of the grammar points introduced in the dialog.

Go to *Active German: Level 1 > Unit 1 > Lesson 1 > Grammar* to listen to these explanations and to access some interactive practice activities.

1 ›   How are you?

To ask somebody how he or she is, there are two different ways in German:

*Formally: **Wie geht es Ihnen?***	How are you?
*Informally: **Wie geht es dir?***	How are you?

2 ›   How are you? I am fine, thank you.

To answer and then ask the question in return, you use:

Formally: **Danke. Gut. Und Ihnen?**	I am fine, thank you. And you?
Informally: **Danke. Gut. Und dir?**	I am fine, thank you. And you?

Culture note   ⓘ

Cologne, with almost one million inhabitants, is Germany's fourth-largest city (after Berlin, Hamburg, and Munich). It is one of the oldest cities in Germany. Cologne lies on the River Rhine. It is very close to Belgium and France and is very well connected to Brussels and Paris. Many tourists visit Cologne to look at the famous *Kölner Dom* (Cologne Cathedral), the first construction of which dates back to the 9th century. Cologne is well known for its beer, called *Kölsch*, which is a very light beer served in small glasses.

3 › **What is your name? The verb *heißen***

In many languages the verb ending changes according to who is doing the action. The patterns of the verb have to be learned.

Let's look at the verb *heißen*:

ich heiße	my name is (literally: I am called)
du heißt	your name is (*informal*)
Sie heißen	your name is (*formal*)

Note that in *heißen* we have the letter *ß* (called *Eszett*) which represents a special form of the letters *ss*. It is pronounced the same way as an *s*.

Ich heiße Matthias Meisinger.
My name is Matthias Meisinger.

4 › **What is your name?**

er heißt	his name is
sie heißt	her name is
Wie heißt du?	What's your name? (*informal*)
Wie heißen Sie?	What's your name? (*formal*)

5 › The verb *kommen*

Let's look at the verb *kommen* (to come):

kommen to come

ich komme	I come
du kommst	you come (*informal*)
Sie kommen	you come (*formal*)
er kommt	he comes
sie kommt	she comes

6 ›

Different forms of "you"

There are different ways of saying "you." If you're talking to a relative or good friend, use the familiar form *du*. If you're talking to an adult whom you don't know well (e.g. your boss) you use the formal *Sie*.

Compare:

Formal: *Wie heißen Sie?*	What's your name?
Informal: *Wie heißt du?*	What's your name?

Note that the formal *Sie* is written with a capital letter.

Mr. Meisinger and Mr. Buschel have just met for the first time. They are using *Sie*.

7 ›

Where from? A question word

In order to ask where somebody is from you would say:

woher?	where from?
Woher kommen Sie?	Where do you come from?

For the answer you use the word *aus* (from).

> *Ich komme aus Deutschland.*
> I'm from Germany.

Note that in order to say "from the USA" you say *aus den USA.*
Similarly, for Turkey, Switzerland, and the Netherlands, you say
aus der Türkei, *aus der Schweiz*, *aus den Niederlanden*.

8 ›   Hello! Greetings

In order to greet other people you use the following phrases:
Until about 10:00 a.m. you say:

> *Guten Morgen!*
> Good morning!

After 10:00 a.m. you say:

> *Guten Tag!*
> Hello! (literally: Good day!)

After 5:00 p.m. you say:

> *Guten Abend!*
> Good evening!

It is also very common just to say:

Hallo!	Hi!
Guten Morgen Herr Meisinger!	Good morning, Mr. Meisinger.
Guten Tag Frau Müller!	Hello, Mrs. Müller.
Guten Abend alle zusammen!	Good evening, everyone.

9 › ## Goodbye!

There are different ways to say "goodbye" in German. Which expression you use depends on the region.

The most common ones are:

Formal: *Auf Wiedersehen*	Goodbye
Informal: *Tschüss*	Bye

These two expressions can be used everywhere.

Vocabulary

In this section you will learn some useful words and expressions from the dialog.

 Go to Active German: Level 1 > Unit 1 > Lesson 1 > Vocabulary to listen to each of the words being pronounced and to access some interactive practice activities.

Titles and nationalities

Herr
Mr.

Herr Buschel kommt aus Österreich.
Mr. Buschel is from Austria.

Mann
man/husband

Das ist Frau Müllers Mann.
That is Mrs. Müller's husband.

Frau
woman/wife

Das ist Frau Müller.
That is Mrs. Müller.

Deutschland
Germany

Deutschland ist in Europa.
Germany is in Europe.

Kanada
Canada

Kanada ist ein Nachbarland von den USA.
Canada is a neighboring country of the USA.

USA
United States

Die USA sind sehr groß.
The USA is very big.

Culture note

The German language offers two ways of addressing people, depending on the situation and the relationship between the speakers. One form – *Sie* (you) – is used with people you don't know and can also be used to maintain a certain level of formality, professional distance, and respect, while the other – *du* (you) – is used with family, friends, and even in informal situations where the speaker wishes to create a sense of familiarity, informality, or complicity.

England/Großbritannien
England/Great Britain

Großbritannien besteht aus Wales, England und Schottland.
Great Britain consists of Wales, England, and Scotland.

Australien
Australia

Australien ist ein Kontinent.
Australia is a continent.

Brasilien
Brazil

Brasilien liegt in Südamerika.
Brazil is in South America.

Österreich
Austria

In Österreich spricht man Deutsch.
In Austria they speak German.

UNIT 1 › LESSON 2
Arrival – At the train station 2

Culture note ⓘ

To greet somebody you normally shake hands. Closer friends and young people may hug each other or even give each other a little kiss. However, if you don't know the person or if it is a professional relationship you should just shake hands.

Video Dialog

· ·

Lara Roellinger introduces herself to Matthias.

 Active German: Level 1 > Unit 1 > Lesson 2 > Video dialog

Herr Buschel:	*Ah, Frau Roellinger.*
Lara:	*Hallo. Guten Tag. Ah, der neue Kollege. Ich heiße Lara Roellinger.*
Matthias:	*La . . . Wie heißen Sie?*
Lara:	*Mein Vorname ist Lara. Lara Roellinger. L-A-R-A R-O-E-L-L-I-N-G-E-R.*
Matthias:	*Ich heiße Matthias Meisinger. Matthias mit -t-t- und -h- und der Nachname ist Meisinger.*
Herr Buschel:	*Ah, hier ist das Auto. Kommen Sie!*

· ·

Mr. Buschel:	Ah, Mrs. Roellinger.
Lara:	Hello. Ah, our new colleague. My name is Lara Roellinger.
Matthias:	Lara... What is your name?
Lara:	Lara is my first name, Lara Roellinger. L-A-R-A R-O-E-L-L-I-N-G-E-R.
Matthias:	My name is Matthias Meisinger. Matthias with *t-t* and *h*, and my last name is Meisinger.
Mr. Buschel:	Ah, here is the car. Let's go!

Grammar

1 › **How to form verbs**

In lesson 1 you learned about the verb *kommen* (to come). Most verbs follow this same pattern. Here are some examples: *trinken* (to drink), *gehen* (to go, to walk), *spielen* (to play), *singen* (to sing), *fragen* (to ask), *machen* (to do, to make)

Ich trinke Kaffee.	I drink coffee.
Du trinkst Kaffee.	You drink coffee.
Er trinkt Kaffee.	He drinks coffee.
Sie trinkt Kaffee.	She drinks coffee.

2 › Some question words

wie?	how?
Wie heißen Sie?	What is your name?
Wie geht es Ihnen?	How are you?
Wie geht es dir?	How are you?

3 › Some question words

was?	what?
Was trinken Sie?	What are you drinking?
wo?	where?
Wo spielt er?	Where is he playing?

4 › **I, you, he, and she**

The subject of a sentence is usually a person or a thing performing the action shown by the verb.

Ich fliege nach Deutschland.
I am flying to Germany.

5 › **I, you, he, and she**

The following words are called pronouns and are used as the subject of a sentence. They represent a person or a thing. The singular pronouns are:

ich	I
du	you (*informal*)
Sie	you (*formal*)
er	he, it
es	it
sie	she, it

6 › **Capital letters**

Note that German nouns are always written with a capital letter.

*Lara ist mein **V**orname.*
Lara is my first name.

*Hier ist das **A**uto.*
Here is the car.

 ## *Vocabulary*

 Active German: Level 1 > Unit 1 > Lesson 2 > Vocabulary

The alphabet

The name of almost every letter in German contains the sound ordinarily represented by that letter. The German alphabet is based on the Latin alphabet but has four additional letters.

a b c
d e f g

a – *ah*   b – *beh*   c – *tseh*
d – *deh*   e – *eh*   f – *eff*
g – *geh*

h i j k l m

h – *hah*   i – *ih*   j – *jott*
k – *kah*   l – *ell*   m – *emm*

n o p q r

n – *enn*   o – *oh*   p – *peh*
q – *kuh*   r – *err*

s t u v w

s – *ess*   t – *teh*   u – *uh*
v – *fau*   w – *weh*

x y z ß ä ö ü

x – *iks*   y – *üppsilon*
z – *tsett*   ß – *ess-tsett*
ä ö ü

ä, *ö* and *ü* are extra letters in the German alphabet. The pair of dots on each letter is called an umlaut and it changes the sound quality.

Vorname
first name

Mein Vorname ist Matthias.
My first name is Matthias.

Familienname / Nachname
last name

Mein Familienname ist Roellinger.
My last name is Roellinger.

Culture note *i*

Germans tend to keep private and professional lives quite separate. However, colleagues of the same age, especially younger people without their own families, like to go for after-work drinks or meals.

2

Lesson 1: Welcome!

- » How to form verbs in plural.
- » How to form the verb *sein* (to be).
- » How to say where you work:
  Ich arbeite bei Waterfront & Co.
- » Vocabulary about jobs and companies.
- » How to understand a small brochure
  about a company.

Lesson 2: The sun is shining!

- » How to ask questions.
- » How to talk about the weather.
- » Vocabulary about the weather.
- » How to write a short letter about the
  weather and your job.

C Collins | Livemocha™

UNIT 2 › LESSON 1
Welcome!

Culture note

Do the Germans live to work? This old saying describes the reputation of the German attitude towards work. Even though it is true, the Germans have learned how to relax as well and the leisure industry is quite advanced. Nevertheless, the work ethic is very strong, and the Germans rank very high among the most hard-working countries (around 41 hours a week) in Europe. But, it's not all work and no play – Germans are able to enjoy up to 30 days off in a year.

Video Dialog

A warm welcome for Matthias as he gets to know his new colleagues a little better.

 Active German: Level 1 > Unit 2 > Lesson 1 > Video dialog

Matthias:	*Arbeiten Sie auch im Marketing?*
Herr Buschel:	*Nein, ich arbeite im Controlling.*
Lara:	*Ich arbeite im Marketing.*
Matthias:	*Ah schön, dann arbeiten wir ja zusammen.*
Herr Buschel:	*Die Firma hat viele Mitarbeiter und ist sehr groß. Herr Baumann, unser Chef, ist sehr nett.*
Lara:	*Alle Kollegen bei Waterfront & Co. sind sehr nett.*
Herr Buschel:	*Wir sind sehr international. Wir arbeiten mit den USA, Japan, China und Mexiko.*
Lara:	*Hier sind wir. Das ist die Firma.*

Matthias:	Do you work in marketing as well?
Mr. Buschel:	No, I work as a controller.
Lara:	I work in the marketing department.
Matthias:	Ah, good, we will be working together then.
Mr. Buschel:	The company has many members of staff and is very big. Mr. Baumann, our boss, is very nice.
Lara:	All colleagues working for Waterfront & Co. are very nice.

| Mr. Buschel: | We are very international. We work with the USA, Japan, China, and Mexico. |
| Lara: | Here we are. This is the company. |

Grammar

Active German: Level 1 > Unit 2 > Lesson 1 > Grammar

1 › **Plural pronouns**

So far we have covered the singular pronouns: *Ich, du, er / sie.*
Here are the plural pronouns:

wir	we
ihr	you (*informal*)
Sie	you (*formal*)
sie	they

2 ›   Lara – she!

Note:

> *Herr Meisinger und Frau Roellinger → sie arbeiten im Marketing.*
> Mr. Meisinger and Mrs. Roellinger → they work in marketing.

> *Frau Roellinger → sie arbeitet*
> she works

> *Herr Meisinger → er arbeitet*
> he works

3 ›   Verbs in plural

So far we have covered the verb endings in the singular: *ich komme, du kommst, er / sie kommt.*

The plural endings take the following pattern:

wir kommen	we come
ihr kommt	you come (*informal*)
Sie kommen	you come (*formal*)
sie kommen	they come

4 › **The verb "to work" (1)**

arbeiten	to work
ich arbeite	I work
du arbeitest	you work
er / sie / es arbeitet	he / she / it works

Ich arbeite im Controlling. Herr Meisinger arbeitet im Marketing.

I work as a controller. Mr. Meisinger works in the marketing department.

Arbeiten has slightly different endings in the *du* and *er / sie* forms than regular verbs.

Compare:

> *du komm**st***   *er / sie komm**t***
> *du arbeit**est***   *er / sie arbeit**et***

5 › **The verb "to work" (2)**

wir arbeiten	we work
ihr arbeitet	you work (*informal*)
Sie arbeiten	you work (*formal*)
sie arbeiten	they work

Arbeiten has a slightly different ending in the *ihr* form than regular verbs.

Compare:

ihr kommt
ihr arbeitet

6 › | I work at Siemens

To say where you work, you use the prepositions *bei* or *für*.

Ich arbeite bei Siemens.
I work at Siemens.

Ich arbeite für BMW.
I work for BMW.

7 › ## Female forms

In German you use the ending *-in* for female forms of nouns:

*Kollege – Kolleg**in***	female colleague
*Lehrer – Lehrer**in***	female teacher

8 › ## I am

The verb *sein* (to be) is irregular. Take some time to memorize its forms.

Singular:

ich bin	I am
du bist	you are
er / sie / es ist	he / she / it is

9 ›

We are

Plural:

wir sind	we are
ihr seid	you are
sie / Sie sind	they / you are

Tip: In German you don't translate the "a" when you talk about your job. *Ich bin Ingenieur.* "I'm an engineer."

 Vocabulary

· ·

 Active German: Level 1 > Unit 2 > Lesson 1 > Vocabulary

Jobs and the company

Chef
boss

Herr Baumann ist der Chef.
Mr. Baumann is the boss.

Kollege
colleague

Das ist mein Kollege.
This is my colleague.

Mitarbeiter
employees

Herr Baumann hat viele Mitarbeiter.
Mr. Baumann has many employees.

Lehrer
teacher

Ich bin Lehrer.
I'm a teacher.

Verkäufer
salesclerk

Er ist Verkäufer.
He is a salesclerk.

Sekretärin
(female) secretary

Herr Baumann hat eine Sekretärin.
Mr. Baumann has a secretary.

Firma
company

Waterfront & Co. ist eine große Firma.
Waterfront & Co. is a big company.

parken
to park

Hier parken wir.
We'll park here.

der Beruf / Berufe*
job, profession

Was sind Sie von Beruf?
What is your profession?

*The plural form of all German nouns has been included next to the singular form. In some cases both forms are identical.

nett
nice

Matthias ist sehr nett.
Matthias is very nice.

UNIT 2 › LESSON 2

The sun is shining!

Culture note ⓘ

The climate in Germany is mainly moderate. Large fluctuations in temperature are rare, even though in some summers the temperature might rise to 95°F (35°C) and in some winters fall to 5°F (−15°C). Rain falls throughout the year. Temperatures vary from east to west and from north to south. The south of Germany is slightly warmer than the north. The north is influenced by the Baltic and North Seas, and a breeze is present most of the time. Summer temperatures are typically between 64° and 86°F (18° and 30°C), and a nice summer might keep beer gardens open through October.

Video Dialog

Matthias gets to know the company before they all go for a
morning coffee.

 Active German: Level 1 > Unit 2 > Lesson 2 > Video dialog

Herr Buschel:	*Wir sind da. Willkommen bei Waterfront & Co. in Pulheim.*
Lara:	*Leider ist es heute nicht so schön. Es ist ein bisschen kalt.*
Matthias:	*Regnet es oft in Pulheim?*
Herr Buschel:	*Ja, leider. In Pulheim ist es aber oft warm.*
Matthias:	*Das Haus ist aber groß!*
Lara:	*Ja, und es ist sehr modern.*
Herr Buschel:	*Und sehr schön. Waterfront & Co. – freundlich und kompetent. Das ist unser Motto.*
Lara:	*Gehen wir erst in ein Café?*
Matthias:	*Ja, gerne.*

....

Mr. Buschel:	Here we are. Welcome to Waterfront & Co. in Pulheim.
Lara:	Unfortunately the weather's not so nice today. It's a bit cold.
Matthias:	Does it often rain in Pulheim?
Mr. Buschel:	Yes, unfortunately. But it is often warm in Pulheim.
Matthias:	What a big building!
Lara:	Yes, and it is very modern.

Mr. Buschel:	And very beautiful. Waterfront & Co. – friendly and competent. That is our motto.
Lara:	Shall we go to a café first?
Matthias:	Yes, with pleasure.

Grammar

1 › **Word order**

In a sentence the verb is normally in position two. This is a very strict word-order rule in German.

| *Ich **arbeite** hier.* | I work here. |
| *Du **trinkst** Kaffee.* | You drink coffee. |

2 › Question words

In unit 1 you saw how to form a question with a question word:

Wo arbeiten Sie?	Where do you work?
Wo sind Sie?	Where are you?
Was trinken Sie?	What do you drink?

3 › Questions

Now you will see how to form a question with a verb. The verb goes at the beginning of the question:

***Arbeiten** Sie bei Waterfront & Co?*	Do you work at Waterfront & Co.?
***Sind** Sie neu hier?*	Are you new here?
***Geht** es Ihnen gut?*	Is everything good with you?

4 › **Answers**

Arbeiten Sie hier?
The answer is *ja* (yes) or *nein* (no).

Arbeiten Sie bei Waterfront & Co?	Do you work at Waterfront & Co.?
Ja, ich arbeite hier.	Yes, I work here.
Nein, ich arbeite bei BMW.	No, I work at BMW.

5 › **The weather**

In order to talk about the weather, very often the word *es* (it) is used along with the form *ist* (is) of the verb *sein* (to be).

Es ist schön.	It is beautiful.
Es ist warm.	It is warm.
Es ist kalt.	It is cold.

6 › ## The weather

When talking about the rain, the verb *regnen* is used.

Es regnet.
It is raining.

When talking about the sun (*die Sonne*) shining, the verb *scheinen* is used.

Die Sonne scheint.
The sun is shining.

Culture note ⓘ

Pulheim is in the northwest of Cologne. With 53,000 inhabitants it is a rather small town. In 1981, however, it was granted city status. It is a fairly typical German *Mittelstadt* (medium-sized town) with a market place, a town hall, and all the necessary stores. Pulheim's beautiful surroundings are perfect for cycling and walking tours.

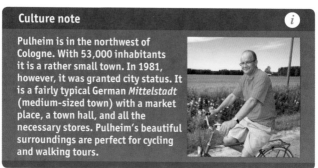

Vocabulary

 Active German: Level 1 > Unit 2 > Lesson 2 > Vocabulary

The weather

schön
beautiful

Heute ist es schön.
Today it is nice.

warm
warm

In München ist es warm.
It is warm in Munich.

heiß
hot

Heute ist es heiß.
It is hot today.

kalt
cold

Es ist kalt.
It is cold.

51

windig
windy

Am Meer ist es sehr windig.
At the seaside it is very windy.

schneien
to snow

Im Winter schneit es oft.
In winter it snows very often.

Frühling
spring

Im Frühling scheint die Sonne.
In spring the sun shines.

Sommer
summer

Im Sommer ist es heiß.
It is hot in summer.

Herbst
fall

Im Herbst ist es oft windig.
It is very windy in fall.

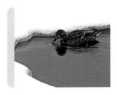

Winter
winter

Im Winter ist es kalt.
In winter it is cold.

3

Lesson 1: In a café 1

» How to get information about drinks and food: *Ist die Suppe gut?*

» About articles: *der Kaffee, die Frau, das Auto.*

» About the verb *kosten.*

» Vocabulary in a café.

Lesson 2: In a café 2

» How to ask for prices: *Was kostet ...?*

» How to count from 0–20.

» About the plural form: e.g. *Hotels, Männer.*

» About a menu in a café.

◯ **Collins** | Live**mocha**™

UNIT 3 › LESSON 1
In a café 1

Culture note

Germany is the second largest market for coffee. At home people normally drink filtered coffee. They drink it either black, with milk (hot or cold) and/or with sugar. Coffee is often enjoyed as an accompaniment to cake (*Kuchen*). In fact, a favorite snack is the afternoon *Kaffee und Kuchen*, a tradition which is enjoyed as part of a social gathering either at home or in a café. Germany has also seen an upsurge in a new coffee culture, and you can select from a wide range of different coffee drinks: café latte, cappuccino, latte macchiato, etc. *Milchkaffee* is the German version of the French *café au lait*.

Video Dialog

In the café, Matthias, Lara, and Mr. Buschel order food and drinks.

 Active German: Level 1 > Unit 3 > Lesson 1 > Video dialog

Lara:	*Ah, der Stuhl ist noch frei.*
Herr Buschel:	*Haben Sie Durst oder Hunger?*
Matthias:	*Ich habe Durst und ein bisschen Hunger.*
Herr Buschel:	*Was trinken Sie?*
Matthias:	*Ich trinke Kaffee und ein Glas Wasser, bitte. Ist die Suppe gut?*
Lara:	*Ja, ja die Suppe ist sehr lecker. Essen Sie Suppe?*
Matthias:	*Ja, gerne.*
Lara:	*Zwei Suppen, bitte.*
Herr Buschel:	*Zwei Suppen, ein Kaffee, ein Glas Wasser und...?*
Lara:	*Ich trinke eine Cola.*

Lara:	Ah, this chair is free.
Mr. Buschel:	Are you thirsty or hungry?
Matthias:	I am thirsty and a little bit hungry.
Mr. Buschel:	What are you having to drink?
Matthias:	I'll have a coffee and a glass of water, please. Is the soup good?

Lara:	Yes, the soup is really good. Are you going to have some?
Matthias:	Yes, please.
Lara:	Two soups, please.
Mr. Buschel:	Two soups, a coffee, a glass of water and...?
Lara:	I'll have a soda.

Grammar

. . . .

 Active German: Level 1 > Unit 3 > Lesson 1 > Grammar

1 › Articles (1)

In German, as in most languages, nouns are not normally used on their own, but are very often preceded by an article (*Artikel*). In German, we have three different articles for "the": *der – die – das*.

2 › Articles (2)

This article is used if there is only one object or person or if something is new or unknown. It normally refers to something particular or something we already know.

> ### Der Stuhl ist da.
> The chair is over there.

3 › *der – die – das* (1)

All German nouns are either masculine (*der*), feminine (*die*), or neuter (*das*):

der Stuhl: Ist der Stuhl frei?	Is the chair free?
die Suppe: Ist die Suppe gut?	Is the soup good?
das Haus: Das Haus ist groß.	The house is big.

4 › **der – die – das (2)**

There is often no logic as to whether a noun is masculine, feminine, or neuter.

One important rule is that grammatical gender usually reflects real gender for words denoting people: *die Frau* (the woman), *der Mann* (the man), *der Kollege* (the male colleague), *die Kollegin* (the female colleague).

5 › Learning tip

It's a good idea to learn the article with the noun when you come across a word for the first time, so that you know whether it is masculine, feminine, or neuter. Some learners like to try to remember the noun by using colors when writing them down, e.g.,

der	blue
die	red
das	yellow

6 › Articles (3)

We use a different article – *ein* (meaning "a") – to refer to any item that is not a specific one.

There are three different forms:

ein	masculine
eine	feminine
ein	neuter

7 › "A" or "the"?

> *Was kostet **der** Kaffee?*
> How much is **the** coffee?

The speaker is referring to a particular coffee.

> ***Ein** Kaffee kostet €2,20.*
> **A** coffee costs €2.20.

This is general information and you are not referring to a particular coffee.

8 › The verb *kosten*

You use the verb *kosten* (to cost) to state prices.

> Singular: *Was kost**et** der Kaffee?*
> How much is the coffee?

> *Plural:* *Was kost**en** die Suppen?*
> How much are the soups?

9 ›   How to read out prices

The word *Euro* is added between the whole number and the cents:

So for €3.20 say: 3 *Euro* 20.

Vocabulary

 Active German: Level 1 > Unit 3 > Lesson 1 > Vocabulary

In a café

der Kaffee / Kaffees
coffee

Der Kaffee kostet 2 Euro.
The coffee costs 2 Euros.

das Café / Cafés
café

Das Café ist sehr nett.
The café is very nice.

der Tee / Tees
tea

Ich trinke gern Tee.
I like drinking tea.

die Suppe / Suppen
soup

Ist die Suppe gut?
Is the soup good?

die Speisekarte/Speisekarten
menu

Ist das die Speisekarte?
Is that the menu?

der Stuhl / Stühle
chair

Ist der Stuhl frei?
Is the chair free?

das Glas / Gläser
glass

Ich trinke ein Glas Wasser.
I'll have a glass of water.

die Tasse / Tassen
cup

Eine Tasse Kaffee, bitte.
A cup of coffee, please.

der Teller / Teller
plate

Hier ist ein Teller mit Kuchen.
Here is a plate of cake.

der Löffel / Löffel
spoon

Wo ist der Löffel für die Suppe?
Where is the spoon for the soup?

UNIT 3 › LESSON 2
In a café 2

Culture note ⓘ

In Germany there are several possibilities for the midday meal at work. It is not unusual to bring your own lunch with you. Bigger companies have their own cafeterias with a variety of hot and cold dishes. It is common to have lunch with your colleagues. In restaurants or cafés there is often a *Mittagstisch* (lunch special).

Video Dialog

· ·

Having finished their meals, it's time to ask for the check.

 Active German: Level 1 > Unit 3 > Lesson 2 > Video dialog

Herr Buschel:	*Hier ist die Suppe.*
Lara:	*Danke.*
Matthias:	*Danke.*
Herr Buschel:	*Eine Cola?*
Lara:	*Ja.*
Matthias:	*Was kostet die Suppe?*
Herr Buschel:	*Mmh, die zwei Suppen kosten €6,20, also kostet eine €3,10.*
Matthias:	*Und was kostet der Kaffee?*
Herr Buschel:	*Der Kaffee kostet €2,15.*
Matthias:	*Und das Wasser?*
Herr Buschel:	*Ach, das Wasser kostet nichts.*
Matthias:	*Hier sind 6 Euro.*
Herr Buschel:	*Nein, nein ich bezahle heute.*
Matthias:	*Danke schön.*

· ·

Mr. Buschel:	Here is the soup.
Lara:	Thanks.
Matthias:	Thanks.
Mr. Buschel:	A soda?

Lara:	Yes.
Matthias:	How much does the soup cost?
Mr. Buschel:	Hmm, two soups cost €6.20, so one costs €3.10.
Matthias:	And how much does the coffee cost?
Mr. Buschel:	The coffee costs €2.15.
Matthias:	And the water?
Mr. Buschel:	Oh, the water doesn't cost anything.
Matthias:	Here are 6 euros.
Mr. Buschel:	No, no, I'll pay today.
Matthias:	Thank you.

Grammar

. . . .

 Active German: Level 1 > Unit 3 > Lesson 2 > Grammar

1 ›   Plurals (1)

Nouns normally have a singular and a plural form. The article indicates this. Fortunately, the plural article is always the same – *die*. It doesn't matter whether the noun is masculine, feminine, or neuter. In German, there are several different ways of making nouns plural.

> *Singular:* **Eine Suppe kostet €3,10.**
> A soup costs €3.10.
>
> *Plural:* **Zwei Suppen kosten €6,20.**
> Two soups cost €6.20.

2 › Plurals (2)

Here are some examples:

Most feminine nouns form their plural by adding -n, -en or -nen to their singular form:

*die Information – die Information**en***	(information / information)
*die Frau – die Frau**en***	(woman / women)
*die Lehrerin – die Lehrerin**nen***	(teacher / teachers)
*die Speisekarte – die Speisekarte**n***	(menu / menus)
*die Suppe – die Suppe**n***	(soup / soups)

3 › Plurals (3)

Some masculine or neuter nouns add -e, -er or umlaut and -er to form their plural:

*der Mann – die M**ä**nn**er***	(man / men)
*das Haus – die H**äu**s**er***	(house / houses)

Some masculine nouns add an umlaut (¨) above the first vowel a, o or u and an -e ending to form the plural:

*der Stuhl – die St**üh**l**e***
(chair / chairs)

4 › **Plurals (4)**

Many nouns have no plural ending. They are mostly masculine or neuter nouns ending in -en, -er or -el.

der Mitarbeiter – die Mitarbeiter	(employee / employees)
der Computer – die Computer	(computer / computers)
der Lehrer – die Lehrer	(teacher / teachers)

Some of these nouns also have an umlaut added to the first vowel a, o or u in the plural:

der Vater – die Väter

(father / fathers)

5 › **Plurals (5)**

There is another group of German nouns (very often words from other languages) which don't follow the rules that have just been mentioned. It is common for such words to form their plural by adding -s.

| *das Hotel – die Hotels* | (hotel / hotels) |
| *der Chef – die Chefs* | (boss / bosses) |

All nouns ending in -o and many ending in -a add an -s as well.

| *das Kino – die Kinos* | (movie theater / movie theaters) |
| *das Auto – die Autos* | (car / cars) |

6 › Plurals (6)

Note that plural verb forms must be used with plural nouns:

> *Das Hotel **ist** gut. – Die Hotels **sind** gut.*
> The hotel is good. – The hotels are good.

 # *Vocabulary*

· ·

Active German: Level 1 > Unit 3 > Lesson 2 > Vocabulary

Numbers and prices

0 1 2 3 4

0 – null
1 – eins
2 – zwei
3 – drei
4 – vier

5 6 7 8 9

5 – fünf
6 – sechs
7 – sieben
8 – acht
9 – neun

10 11 12
13 14 15

10 – *zehn*
11 – *elf*
12 – *zwölf*
13 – *dreizehn*
14 – *vierzehn*
15 – *fünfzehn*

16 17
18 19 20

16 – *sechzehn*
17 – *siebzehn*
18 – *achtzehn*
19 – *neunzehn*
20 – *zwanzig*

der Euro
euro

In Deutschland bezahlt man mit Euro.
In Germany you pay in euros.

der Cent
cent

Das kostet 3 Euro und 20 Cent.
That costs 3 euros 20 cents.

4

Lesson 1: The new home

» How to form sentences such as "I have an apartment."
» Vocabulary about the different rooms in an apartment or house.
» How to talk about your apartment.
» How to express whether you like your apartment or not.
» About the verb *haben* (to have).

Lesson 2: In the apartment

» How to talk about an apartment and say what you have and what you need: *Ich habe einen Schrank, Ich brauche die Telefonnummer*.
» How to use the verbs *brauchen* (to need) and *kaufen* (to buy).
» Vocabulary about your apartment and objects in daily life.

☼ Collins | **Livemocha™**

UNIT 4 › LESSON 1
The new home

Culture note ⓘ

Gemütlichkeit (coziness) is a very important concept in German. This term describes more than just a warm and nicely furnished place; it conveys the notion of quality and satisfaction. Finding this cozy place to live is not always easy, and finding good accommodation can be hard, especially in large cities. It is very common for people under 40 in Germany to rent an apartment. Young people like to share apartments and live in so called WGs (*Wohngemeinschaften* – shared housing).

Video Dialog

When Lara asks Matthias about his new apartment, he invites her to come and see what it's like for herself.

 Active German: Level 1 > Unit 4 > Lesson 1 > Video dialog

Matthias:	*Danke schön.*
Lara:	*Wo wohnen Sie eigentlich?*
Matthias:	*Ich habe eine Wohnung in Brauweiler.*
Lara:	*Ist das im Osten, bei einem Park?*
Matthias:	*Ja, ich wohne in der Bebelstraße.*
Lara:	*Ist die Wohnung schön?*
Matthias:	*Ja, ich finde meine Wohnung schön. Ich habe zwei Zimmer – ein Wohnzimmer und ein Schlafzimmer – ein Badezimmer und natürlich eine Küche.*
Lara:	*Gut. Haben Sie einen Balkon oder einen Garten?*
Matthias:	*Ich habe einen Balkon.*
Lara:	*Ist die Wohnung teuer?*
Matthias:	*Na ja, die Wohnung ist nicht teuer und nicht billig. Die Miete ist OK. Und die Lage ist ganz wunderbar. Ein Supermarkt ist direkt um die Ecke. Besuchen Sie mich doch mal!*

Matthias:	Thank you.
Lara:	Tell me, where do you live?
Matthias:	I have an apartment in Brauweiler.
Lara:	Is that in the east, near a park?
Matthias:	Yes, I live in Bebelstraße.
Lara:	Is it a nice apartment?
Matthias:	Yes, I think my apartment is very nice. I have two rooms – a living room and a bedroom – a bathroom and a kitchen, of course.
Lara:	Good. Do you have a balcony or a garden?
Matthias:	I have a balcony.
Lara:	Is the apartment expensive?
Matthias:	Well, it's not expensive and not cheap. The rent is OK. And the location is great. A supermarket is just around the corner. Come and visit me!

Grammar

· ·

 Active German: Level 1 > Unit 4 > Lesson 1 > Grammar

1 › | **The nominative case (1)**

A case shows you the function or role of a noun in a sentence. So far you have learned the forms and functions of the nominative case. The nominative case is used for the subject (a person, animal or thing) which is *doing* the action:

> ***Der Mann*** *arbeitet.*
> The man is working.

2 › The nominative case (2)

The nominative case is always used after *sein* (to be), *werden* (to become), and *bleiben* (to stay, to remain).

> ### *Herr Beier ist der Chef.*
> Mr. Beier is the boss.

Der, die, das and *ein, eine, ein* are the articles in the nominative case.

3 › The accusative case

Matthias trinkt einen Kaffee.
Matthias drinks a coffee.

In this sentence the doer of the action "drink" is Matthias and the person or thing affected by the action is the coffee. Matthias is the subject of the sentence and the coffee is the object.

Matthias hat eine Wohnung.
Matthias has an apartment.

In the second example again Matthias is the subject – the doer – and this time the apartment is the object.

4 › "I have an apartment." The accusative case

The case of the object in a sentence is the accusative case. The articles in the accusative case are identical to the nominative, with the exception of their masculine forms.

> *Das ist **eine** Wohnung. – Ich habe **eine** Wohnung.*
> This is an apartment. – I have an apartment.
> *Das ist **ein** Zimmer. – Ich habe **ein** Zimmer.*
> This is a room. – I have a room.
> *Das ist **ein** Balkon. – Ich habe **einen** Balkon.*
> This is a balcony. – I have a balcony.

5 › The verb *haben*

Haben (to have) is a very frequently used verb in German. The forms are slightly irregular.

haben

ich habe	I have
du hast	you have
er, sie, es hat	he, she, it has
wir haben	we have
ihr habt	you have
sie, Sie haben	they, you have

6 › The verb *haben*

Haben requires an object that is in the accusative case. It is a verb expressing that someone has something. The sentence must have a second noun to complete the meaning.

masculine: *Ich habe ein**en** Balkon.*
I have a balcony.

feminine: *Ich habe eine Küche.*
I have a kitchen.

neuter: *Ich habe ein Badezimmer.*
I have a bathroom.

Another example of a verb with an object in the accusative is *trinken*:

> ### Ich trinke einen Tee.
> I drink a cup of tea.

 ## Vocabulary

 Active German: Level 1 > Unit 4 > Lesson 1 > Vocabulary

Living

die Wohnung / Wohnungen
apartment

Ich habe eine Wohnung in Berlin.
I have an apartment in Berlin.

das Zimmer / Zimmer
room

Meine Wohnung hat 3 Zimmer.
My apartment has 3 rooms.

das Badezimmer / Badezimmer
bathroom

Hast du ein Badezimmer und eine Toilette?
Do you have a bathroom and a toilet?

die Küche / Küchen
kitchen

Wo ist die Küche?
Where is the kitchen?

das Schlafzimmer / Schlafzimmer
bedroom

Das Schlafzimmer ist gemütlich.
The bedroom is cozy.

der Balkon / Balkone
balcony

Wir haben einen Balkon und einen Garten.
We have a balcony and a garden.

der Garten / Gärten
garden

Der Garten ist schön!
The garden is beautiful.

die Toilette / Toiletten
toilet

Entschuldigung, wo sind die Toiletten?
Excuse me, where are the toilets?

klein
small

Die Wohnung ist klein, aber gemütlich.
The apartment is small, but cozy.

teuer
expensive

Die Wohnung ist teuer.
The apartment is expensive.

Culture note

Nearly 82 million people live in Germany. Germany has the largest population of all the countries in the European Union and is one of the most densely populated countries in Europe.

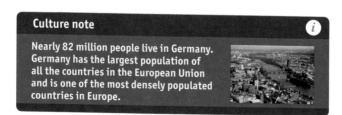

UNIT 4 › LESSON 2
In the apartment

Culture note ⓘ

In Germany it is common to rent an empty apartment, without any furniture at all. Apart from a stove and a washing machine the tenants have to bring their own furniture and electrical appliances.

Video Dialog

Matthias shows Lara around his apartment. Lara asks what furniture Matthias still needs and the two exchange phone numbers.

 Active German: Level 1 > Unit 4 > Lesson 2 > Video dialog

Matthias:	*Und das ist die Küche.*
Lara:	*Ah, einen Kühlschrank und einen Herd haben Sie. Haben Sie schon alle Möbel?*
Matthias:	*Nein, ich brauche noch einen Schrank für das Schlafzimmer. Den Schrank kaufe ich morgen.*
Lara:	*Haben Sie eine Toilette und ein Badezimmer?*
Matthias:	*Ja.*
Lara:	*Ich brauche Ihre Telefonnummer noch.*
Matthias:	*Haben Sie einen Stift?*
Lara:	*Moment. Wo habe ich den Stift? Ja.*
Matthias:	*Meine Telefonnummer ist: 032*
Lara:	*032*
Matthias:	*57*
Lara:	*57*
Matthias:	*88*

Lara:	*88*
Matthias:	*70*
Lara:	*70. Danke.*
Matthias:	*Gerne.*

....

Matthias:	And this is the kitchen.
Lara:	Ah, you have a fridge and a stove. Do you already have all your furniture?
Matthias:	No, I still need a closet for the bedroom. I am going to buy one tomorrow.
Lara:	Do you have a toilet and a bathroom?
Matthias:	Yes.
Lara:	I need your phone number.
Matthias:	Do you have a pen?
Lara:	Hold on. Where is my pen? Yes.
Matthias:	My number is: 032
Lara:	032
Matthias:	57
Lara:	57
Matthias:	88
Lara:	88
Matthias:	70
Lara:	70. Thank you.
Matthias:	You're welcome.

Culture note ⓘ

German is famous for its long words. The language allows you to add as many words as you want to a noun. One of the most famous ones is: *Donaudampfschifffahrtsgesellschaftskapitän*, which in English is: "Danube steamship company captain." This German word has 42 letters, while some others are even longer.

Grammar

Active German: Level 1 > Unit 4 > Lesson 2 > Grammar

1 › **The accusative case**

In lesson 1 we learned about the noun as an object with the article "a" (*einen, eine, ein* – indefinite article). Let's have a look now at the noun as object with "the" (definite article). The article in the accusative case is very similar to the nominative case. The only difference is the masculine form.

Nominative	Accusative
Masculine: Hier ist der Kaffee. Here is the coffee.	*Der Mann trinkt **den Kaffee.*** The man drinks the coffee.
Feminine: Hier ist die Cola. Here is the soda.	*Frau Roellinger trinkt **die Cola.*** Mrs. Roellinger drinks the soda.
Neuter: Hier ist das Wasser. Here is the water.	*Die Frau trinkt **das Wasser.*** The woman drinks the water.
Plural: Hier sind die Stühle. Here are the chairs.	*Wir haben **die Stühle.*** We have the chairs.

2 › ## Whom?

The question word *wer* or *was* (who or what) in the nominative case is used for the person or thing that is doing something. The accusative form of the question word *wer* is *wen* (whom). *Was* (what) remains the same in both nominative and accusative cases.

Wer ist das?	Who is that?
Das ist der Mann von Frau Schulz.	That is the husband of Mrs. Schulz.
Wen kennst du?	Whom do you know?
Ich kenne den Mann von Frau Schulz.	I know the husband of Mrs. Schulz.

3 › ## The verb *brauchen*

Ich brauche einen Schrank.
I need a closet.

The verb *brauchen* requires the accusative case as well. In the sentence *Ich brauche einen Schrank – Ich* is the subject and *einen Schrank* the object.

4 › **The verb *kaufen***

The verb *kaufen* (to buy) and many other verbs require an object in the accusative:

> ### *Ich kaufe eine Flasche Wein.*
> I buy a bottle of wine. (*eine* is in the accusative case)

5 › **Verbs with accusative**

So far we have seen four verbs with the accusative: *trinken* (to drink), *haben* (to have), *kaufen* (to buy), and *brauchen* (to need).

Let's look at another example – *suchen* (to look for, to search).

Wen suchst du?	Who (Whom) are you looking for?
Den Chef.	The boss.
Wer sucht den Chef?	Who is looking for the boss?
Ich.	I am.

Vocabulary

 Active German: Level 1 > Unit 4 > Lesson 2 > Vocabulary

Furniture and useful objects

die Waschmaschine / Waschmaschinen
washing machine

Die Waschmaschine ist kaputt.
The washing machine is broken.

der Schrank / Schränke
closet

Heute kaufe ich einen Schrank.
Today I'm going to buy a closet.

der Herd / Herde
stove

Der Herd ist in der Küche.
The stove is in the kitchen.

die Möbel
furniture

Ich kaufe meine Möbel bei IKEA.
I buy my furniture in IKEA.

der Schlüssel / Schlüssel
key

Wo sind meine Schlüssel?
Where are my keys?

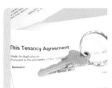

der Vertrag / Verträge
contract

Ich unterschreibe den Vertrag.
I sign the contract.

die Telefonnummer / Telefonnummern
phone number

Meine Telefonnummer ist 040/348827.
My phone number is 040/348827

der Stift / Stifte
pen

Hast du einen Stift?
Do you have a pen?

die Miete / Mieten
rent

Ich bezahle 500 Euro Miete im Monat.
I pay rent of 500 euros a month.

das Bett / Betten
bed

Mein Schlafzimmer ist klein, aber mein Bett ist groß.
My bedroom is small, but my bed is big.

5

Lesson 1: My new office

» How to say what belongs to you and others: ***Das ist mein Buch, Ist das Ihre Tasse?***

» Vocabulary for the office and the working world.

» Eliciting information from advertisements.

Lesson 2: At work

» How to give basic personal information about yourself.

» How to say that you don't do something: ***Ich arbeite nicht, ich habe keine Kinder***.

» Vocabulary for personal details: ***Meine Adresse, meine Handynummer***.

» How to fill out a simple form.

© Collins | Livemocha™

UNIT 5 › LESSON 1
My new office

Culture note ⓘ

You'll find many English words in a German office. Most of the
time these words are related to technology, and English words
have been adopted in the language when there has been the
need to name new inventions, e.g., *der Computer*, *der Scanner*,
die Email or new verbs such as *downloaden*. In addition, German
has often taken English words and given them a completely
different meaning e.g. *das Handy* for cell phone or *der Beamer*
for data projector. Some Germans don't even know that these
words are not the same in English!

Video Dialog

Back at work, Matthias meets Mr. Baumann and settles into his new office.

 Active German: Level 1 > Unit 5 > Lesson 1 > Video dialog

Matthias:	*Guten Morgen, Herr Baumann. Wie geht es Ihnen?*
Herr Baumann:	*Sehr gut. Und Ihnen?*
Matthias:	*Gut, alles ist neu. Das ist sehr interessant.*
Herr Baumann:	*Ja, ja, Sie sind noch jung, da ist alles neu. Schauen Sie, das ist Ihr Büro. Das ist Ihr Schreibtisch und alles, was Sie brauchen. Unser Drucker ist dort.*
Matthias:	*Ist das Ihr Büro rechts?*
Herr Baumann:	*Nein, mein Büro ist oben. Viel Glück und viel Spaß!*
Matthias:	*Gut, danke. Mmh. Mein Schreibtisch, mein Computer und mein Telefon.*

....

Matthias:	Good morning, Mr. Baumann. How are you?
Mr. Baumann:	Very good. And you?
Matthias:	Good, everything is new. It is very interesting.
Mr. Baumann:	Yes, yes, you are still young. Everything is new then. Have a look. This is your office. This is your desk and everything else that you'll need. Our printer is over there.

Matthias:	Is that your office on the right?
Mr. Baumann:	No, my office is upstairs. Good luck and enjoy!
Matthias:	Good, thank you. Hmm. My desk, my computer and my phone.

 # Grammar

. . . .

Active German: Level 1 > Unit 5 > Lesson 1 > Grammar

1 › My office

> ### *Das ist **Ihr** Schreibtisch.*
> This is your desk.

> ### *Das ist **mein** Büro.*
> This is my office.

Mein (my), *unser* (our), *Ihr* (your) and *sein* (his) are adjectives to indicate possession. They tell us what belongs to whom.

2 ›
My office

In German these adjectives change according to the gender of the noun.

Masculine	*ein Mann → mein Mann*	my husband
Feminine	*eine Frau → meine Frau*	my wife
Neuter	*ein Büro → mein Büro*	my office
Plural	*Stifte → meine Stifte*	my pens

3 ›
Your office

The form of the German for "my," "your," "his," "her," and "our" depends on the gender of the noun.

my

mein Chef	my boss
meine Wohnung	my apartment
mein Büro	my office
meine Stifte	my pens (*plural*)

your

dein Chef	your boss
deine Wohnung	your apartment
dein Büro	your office
deine Stifte	your pens
Ist das dein Chef?	Is that your boss?

4 › ### Her office

These are the words for "his" and "her":

his

sein Chef	his boss
seine Wohnung	his apartment
sein Büro	his office
seine Stifte	his pens
Das ist seine Telefonnummer.	That is his phone number.

her

ihr Chef	her boss
ihre Wohnung	her apartment
ihr Büro	her office
ihre Stifte	her pens
Das ist ihr Mann.	That is her husband.

5 › Our office

our

unser Chef	our boss
unsere Wohnung	our apartment
unser Büro	our office
Unser Chef ist sehr nett.	Our boss is very nice.

6 › Your office

When you address someone formally you use the following form:

your (formal)

Ihr Chef	your boss
Ihre Wohnung	your apartment
Ihr Büro	your office
Ist das Ihr Kaffee, Herr Meisinger?	Is that your coffee, Mr. Meisinger?

7 › **Note the difference**

*Das ist **ihr** Haus.*
It is her house.

*Das ist **Ihr** Haus.*
It is your house. This could be singular or plural. In this case *Ihr* has a capital letter.

 # *Vocabulary*

Active German: Level 1 > Unit 5 > Lesson 1 > Vocabulary

Office and personal information

der Schreibtisch / Schreibtische
desk

Mein Schreibtisch ist sehr groß.
My desk is very big.

das Büro / Büros
office

Wo ist Ihr Büro?
Where is your office?

das Telefon / Telefone
phone

Mein Telefon ist kaputt.
My phone is broken.

das Handy / Handys
cell phone

Heute kaufe ich ein Handy.
Today I'm buying a cell phone.

die Telefonnummer / Telefonnummern
phone number

Entschuldigung, wie ist Ihre Telefonnummer?
Excuse me, what is your phone number?

der Computer / Computer
computer

Ich brauche einen Computer.
I need a computer.

das Buch / Bücher
book

Das sind alle Bücher von Goethe.
These are all books by Goethe.

die Post
mail

Ist das meine Post?
Is that my mail?

der Drucker / Drucker
printer

Ist der Drucker neu?
Is the printer new?

jung
young

Matthias ist noch jung.
Matthias is still young.

UNIT 5 › LESSON 2
At work

Culture note ⓘ

Nowadays Germany, like other developed countries, records fewer marriages, more divorces, and fewer children. Although the number of single households is increasing all the time, people still get married, especially in times of financial crisis. Interestingly, educational achievement is a crucial factor for determining the age at which people get married: the higher the education, the older couples are when they get married. Yearlong engagements used to be common, but nowadays many couples who get married do so without getting officially engaged beforehand.

Video Dialog

....

Matthias has some forms to fill out at work.

 Active German: Level 1 > Unit 5 > Lesson 2 > Video dialog

Lara:	*Hallo.*
Matthias:	*Hallo.*
Lara:	*Wir brauchen ein paar Informationen von Ihnen. Das ist für die Personalabteilung. Brauchen Sie Hilfe?*
Matthias:	*Nein, ich brauche keine Hilfe. Ah, ich habe meine Postleitzahl nicht im Kopf.*
Lara:	*Kein Problem. Das machen wir später.*
Matthias:	*Danke. Also, männlich, weiblich. Ok, das ist einfach. Mein Familienname ist Meisinger, mein Vorname ist Matthias. Familienstand: Nein, ich bin nicht verheiratet, ich bin ledig. Kinder, nein ich habe keine Kinder. Meine Adresse: Bebelstraße 33. Meine Telefonnummer ist: 032 578870. Meine Handynummer ist 0173 452345. Alter: Ich bin 31 Jahre alt. Das ist alles.*

....

Lara:	Hello.
Matthias:	Hello.
Lara:	We need some information from you. It is for Human Resources. Do you need help?

Matthias:	No, I don't need help. Ah, I can't remember my zip code.
Lara:	No problem. We'll do it later.
Matthias:	Thank you. Well, male, female. OK, that's easy. My family name is Meisinger, my first name is Matthias. Family status: no, I am not married, I am single. Children: no, I don't have children. My address is: Bebelstraße 33. My phone number is: 032 578870. My cell number is: 0173 452345. Age: I am 31 years old. That's it.

Grammar

 Active German: Level 1 > Unit 5 > Lesson 2 > Grammar

1 › **How to say no! (1)**

To say that you don't do something, you use the word *nicht*. *Nicht* is used with verbs and makes the sentence negative.

> ### *Ich arbeite **nicht**.*
> I'm not working.

2 › **I'm not Mr. Müller!**

Nicht can follow the verb:

*Er ist **nicht** mein Chef.*	He is not my boss.
*Ich bin **nicht** verheiratet.*	I am not married.
*Es regnet **nicht**.*	It is not raining.
*Ich bin **nicht** Herr Müller.*	I am not Mr. Müller.

115

3 › **How to say no! (2)**

Nicht can follow the object:

> ### Ich benutze den Drucker **nicht**.
> I don't use the printer.

or the subject:

> ### Arbeitest du **nicht**?
> Don't you work?

4 › **How to say no! (3)**

The word *nicht* applies to verbs. When you want to make a negative statement about a noun, you must use *kein*.

Compare:

Ich arbeite nicht.	I don't work.
Ich habe keine Kinder.	I don't have children.

5 › **How to say no! (4)**

Kein is the negative form of *ein*. It takes the same endings as *ein* in the nominative case:

Das ist ein Herd.	*Das ist kein Herd.*	That is not a stove.
Das ist eine Lösung.	*Das ist keine Lösung.*	That is not a solution.
Das ist ein Problem.	*Das ist kein Problem.*	That is not a problem.

6 ›   **How to say no!**

How to make the object of a sentence negative:

Ich habe einen Computer.	*Ich habe keinen Computer.*	I don't have a computer.
Ich habe eine Mikrowelle.	*Ich habe keine Mikrowelle.*	I don't have a microwave.
Ich habe ein Haus.	*Ich habe kein Haus.*	I don't have a house.

Note that there is a plural form of *kein* (no):

> **Ich habe keine Kinder.**
> I don't have children.

Vocabulary

• •

Active German: Level 1 > Unit 5 > Lesson 2 > Vocabulary

Personal information

die Postleitzahl / Postleitzahlen
zip code, postal code

Meine Postleitzahl ist 21 768.
My zip code is 21 768.

das Kind / Kinder
child

Ich habe drei Kinder.
I have three children.

verheiratet
married

Sind Sie verheiratet?
Are you married?

ledig
single

Ich bin ledig.
I'm single.

die Adresse / Adressen
address

Wie ist Ihre Adresse?
What is your address?

das Jahr / Jahre
year

Ich bin 32 Jahre alt.
I'm 32 years old.

das Problem / Probleme
problem

Ich brauche Ihre Hilfe. Ich habe ein Problem.
I need your help. I have a problem.

die Handynummer / Handynummern
cell phone number

Wie ist Ihre Handynummer?
What is your cell phone number?

die Straße / Straßen
street / road

Entschuldigung, wo ist die Bebelstraße?
Excuse me, where is Bebelstraße?

der Familienstand
marital status

Wie ist Ihr Familienstand?
What is your marital status?

6

Lesson 1: An appointment

- » How to ask the time.
- » How to say what time it is.
- » How to count above 20.
- » Vocabulary for dates and times.
- » How to extract information from a calendar.

Lesson 2: A dinner

- » How to form the verbs *lesen, essen, sehen*, and *sprechen*.
- » How to say what you like and what you don't like.
- » Vocabulary for dining with friends.

◯ **Collins** | Live**mocha**™

UNIT 6 › LESSON 1
An appointment

Culture note ⓘ

Germany is part of the Central European time (CET) zone. That means that clocks are ticking 6 hours ahead of Eastern Standard Time (EST) in the United States and 1 hour ahead of Greenwich Mean Time (GMT).

New-York   London   Moscow

Paris   Sydney   Tokyo

Video Dialog

Matthias tries to find a free space in his datebook for an appointment with Mr. Baumann.

 Active German: Level 1 > Unit 6 > Lesson 1 > Video dialog

Herr Baumann:	*Wir brauchen einen Termin für das neue Projekt. Haben Sie am Montag Zeit?*
Matthias:	*Am Montag passt es nicht so gut. Am Morgen habe ich einen Termin mit der Firma Baulitz und am Nachmittag habe ich einen Termin von 15:00 bis 16:00 Uhr.*
Herr Baumann:	*Um 16:00 Uhr habe ich einen Termin. Mmh. Danach fliege ich nach London.*
Matthias:	*Von wann bis wann sind Sie in London?*
Herr Baumann:	*Von Dienstag bis Donnerstag.*
Matthias:	*Um wie viel Uhr kommen Sie zurück?*
Herr Baumann:	*Am Morgen, um 10:30 Uhr.*
Matthias:	*Geht es um 12:00 Uhr?*
Herr Baumann:	*12.00 Uhr ist wunderbar. Oh, es ist schon 18:15. Das Kino beginnt in 30 Minuten. Also bis Donnerstag.*
Matthias:	*Tschüss.*

....

Mr. Baumann:	We need a meeting for our new project. Are you free on Monday?

Matthias:	Monday's not so good. In the morning I have a meeting with the Baulitz company and in the afternoon I have a meeting from 3 p.m. to 4 p.m.
Mr. Baumann:	At 4 o'clock I have a meeting. Afterwards I'm flying to London.
Matthias:	How long are you going to be in London?
Mr. Baumann:	From Tuesday through Thursday.
Matthias:	What time do you get back?
Mr. Baumann:	In the morning, at 10:30.
Matthias:	Does 12 o'clock work for you?
Mr. Baumann:	12 o'clock is great. Oh, it's already 6:15. The movie starts in 30 minutes. See you Thursday.
Matthias:	Bye.

Grammar

 Active German: Level 1 > Unit 6 > Lesson 1 > Grammar

1 › **What time is it? Telling the time (1)**

In everyday speech the 12-hour clock is used, whereas in official contexts the 24-hour clock is used.

Es ist ein Uhr / Es ist eins.	It is one (o'clock).
Es ist 13 Uhr.	It is one p.m.
Es ist drei Uhr.	It is three (o'clock).
Es ist 15 Uhr.	It is three p.m.

2 ›   What time is it? Telling the time (2)

Es ist zehn nach drei.	It is ten past three.
Es ist 15 Uhr 10.	It is 3:10 p.m.
Es ist Viertel nach drei.	It is quarter past three.
Es ist 15 Uhr 15.	It is 3:15 p.m.
Es ist halb vier.	It is half past three
Es ist 15 Uhr 30.	It is 3:30 p.m.

Take note:
halb vier in German means "half of the 4th hour," i.e. 3:30.

3 ›   What time is it? Telling the time (3)

Es ist zwanzig vor vier.	It is twenty to four.
Es ist 15 Uhr 40.	It is 3:40 p.m.
Es ist Viertel vor vier.	It is quarter to four.
Es ist 15 Uhr 45.	It is 3:45 p.m.
Es ist zehn vor vier.	It is ten to four.
Es ist 15 Uhr 50.	It is 3:50 p.m.

4 › **What time is it? Telling the time (4)**

If you want to ask the time you can use the following phrases.

Wie spät ist es?	What time is it? (literally: How late is it?)
Wie viel Uhr ist es?	What time is it? (literally: How many hours is it?)
Es ist 13 Uhr.	It is 1 o'clock.

5 › **When? (1)**

You use the question word *wann* (meaning "when") to ask about a specific moment in time.

Wann fliegen Sie nach London?	When do you fly to London?
Ich fliege am Montag.	I'm flying on Monday.

6 › **When? (2)**

You use the preposition *am* for days and parts of the day and the preposition *im* for months.

am Morgen	in the morning
am Montag	on Monday
im Oktober	in October

7 ›

When? (3)

You use the preposition *um* to refer to a specific time.

Wann kommst du?	When are you coming?
*Ich komme **um** 13 Uhr.*	I'm coming at 1 o'clock.

8 ›

How to express a time period

You use *von wann* to ask for the beginning of the time period and *bis wann* for the end of the time period.

Von wann bis wann sind Sie in London?	How long are you going to be in London? (literally "from when until when")
Von Dienstag bis Donnerstag.	From Tuesday till Thursday.
Von wann bis wann ist unser Termin?	From when until when is our appointment?
Von 9 bis 13 Uhr.	From 9 to 1 o'clock.

9 › **Numbers between 20 and 30**

To read numbers above 20 you start with the second number and follow with the first number.

So: 21 is *ein-und-zwanzig*

21	*einundzwanzig*
22	*zweiundzwanzig*
23	*dreiundzwanzig*
24	*vierundzwanzig*
25	*fünfundzwanzig*
26	*sechsundzwanzig*
27	*siebenundzwanzig*
28	*achtundzwanzig*
29	*neunundzwanzig*

10 › **Numbers between 30 and 200**

The numbers above 30 are formed the same way.

These are the numbers up to 200:

30	*dreißig*
40	*vierzig*
50	*fünfzig*
60	*sechzig*
70	*siebzig*
80	*achtzig*
90	*neunzig*
100	*hundert*
200	*zweihundert*

Vocabulary

· ·

Active German: Level 1 > Unit 6 > Lesson 1 > Vocabulary

Days and months

Montag
Monday

Am Montag habe ich einen Termin.
I have an appointment on Monday.

Dienstag
Tuesday

Morgen ist Dienstag.
Tomorrow is Tuesday.

Mittwoch
Wednesday

Herr Mayer kommt am Mittwoch.
Mr. Mayer is coming on Wednesday.

Donnerstag
Thursday

Am Donnerstag gehe ich ins Kino.
On Thursday I'm going to the movies.

Freitag
Friday

Kommt sie am Freitag?
Is she coming on Friday?

Samstag
Saturday

Am Samstag fliege ich nach London.
On Saturday I'm flying to London.

Sonntag
Sunday

Am Sonntag arbeite ich nicht.
On Sunday I'm not working.

das Wochenende / Wochenenden
weekend

Am Wochenende kommt meine Frau.
My wife is coming this weekend.

Januar
January

Im Januar schneit es manchmal.
In January it sometimes snows.

Februar
February

Im Februar ist Karneval.
Carnival takes place in February.

März
March

Kommen Sie im März zurück?
Are you coming back in March?

April
April

Regnet es oft im April?
Does it often rain in April?

Mai
May

Der Mai ist sehr schön.
May is very nice.

Juni
June

Im Juni beginnt der Sommer.
In June summer begins.

Juli
July

Im Juli ist es heiß.
It is hot in July.

August
August

Im August fliege ich nach Italien.
In August I'm flying to Italy.

September
September

Ist es im September noch sonnig?
Is it still sunny in September?

Oktober
October

Ich habe den Test im Oktober.
I have the test in October.

November
November

Im November regnet es oft.
In November it often rains.

Dezember
December

Weihnachten ist im Dezember.
Christmas is in December.

Culture note ⓘ

The world sometimes laughs at the Germans for their punctuality and their constant clock-watching. But are modern Germans really so punctual? According to a recent study only 18% of Germans still believe in strict timekeeping. Even trains are well-known for being late nowadays. Nevertheless, punctuality is very much appreciated, especially for official meetings. If you realize you are not going to arrive somewhere at the appointed time, you should call and advise that you will be late.

UNIT 6 › LESSON 2
A dinner

Culture note *i*

Germans like to have little dinner parties. But before they invite you to their home for a private dinner, they prefer meeting in a pub or restaurant first. If you are invited to a German person's house, you should bring a gift such as chocolates, wine, or flowers.

137

Video Dialog

. . . .

Lara visits Matthias again and brings a welcome gift before the two get to know one another a little better.

Active German: Level 1 > Unit 6 > Lesson 2 > Video dialog

Lara:	*Entschuldigung, ich bin ein bisschen spät.*
Matthias:	*Kein Problem.*
Lara:	*Die Pralinen sind für Sie.*
Matthias:	*Oh, wie nett, danke schön. Bitte. Trinken Sie Wein?*
Lara:	*Ja, gerne.*
Matthias:	*Warum sagen wir nicht „du" zueinander?*
Lara:	*Gerne.*
Matthias:	*Zum Wohl.*
Lara:	*Zum Wohl. Sie, ich meine du, liest gerne?*
Matthias:	*Ja, sehr gerne.*
Lara:	*Ich lese auch sehr gerne.*
Matthias:	*Isst du gerne Reis?*
Lara:	*Ja, sehr gerne.*
Matthias:	*Es gibt Reis mit Huhn und Salat.*

. . . .

Lara:	Sorry, I'm a bit late.
Matthias:	No problem.
Lara:	The chocolates are for you.

Matthias:	Oh, how nice of you, thank you. Please. Would you like wine?
Lara:	Yes, please.
Matthias:	Why don't we say "du" to each other?
Lara:	With pleasure.
Matthias:	Cheers.
Lara:	Cheers. Do you like reading?
Matthias:	Yes, very much.
Lara:	I like reading as well.
Matthias:	Do you like rice?
Lara:	Yes, very much.
Matthias:	We're having rice with chicken and salad.

Grammar

....

 Active German: Level 1 > Unit 6 > Lesson 2 > Grammar

1 › **More on verbs**

Some German verbs are irregular and they have a different pattern of endings.

In the case of *lesen* (to read) the vowel -e is replaced by -ie in the *du* and *er / sie / es* form.

> ### lesen
> to read

singular:

ich lese	I read
*du **lie**st*	you read
*er / sie / es **lie**st*	he / she / it reads

139

2 › The verb *lesen*

The plural follows the normal pattern.

wir lesen	we read
ihr lest	you read
sie, Sie lesen	they read, you read
Lara liest gerne.	Lara likes reading.

3 › More on verbs

The verbs *sehen* (to see) and *essen* (to eat) follow the same
pattern as the verb *lesen*.

Wen siehst du?	Whom do you see?
Er isst gerne Reis.	He likes eating rice.

4 › **The verb *sprechen***

The verb *sprechen* (to speak) has a change of vowel as well.

> ### *sprechen*
> to speak

singular:

ich spreche	I speak
du sprichst	you speak
er / sie / es spricht	he / she / it speaks
Katja spricht Spanisch	Katja speaks Spanish.

5 › **The verb *sprechen***

plural:

wir sprechen	we speak
ihr sprecht	you speak
sie, Sie sprechen	they speak, you speak

6 › **What do you like?**

In German, in order to express that you like to do something you use the verb + *gern* or *gerne*

Ich lese gern.	I like reading.
Essen Sie gern Fisch?	Do you like eating fish?

To make *gern* negative say *nicht gern* (I don't like doing).

> ### *Ich arbeite nicht gern.*
> I don't like working.

Vocabulary

Active German: Level 1 > Unit 6 > Lesson 2 > Vocabulary

Dinner and food

zum Wohl or *Prost*
Cheers

In Deutschland sagt man „Zum Wohl" oder „Prost".
In Germany you say "Cheers."

das Essen
food

Ist das Essen fertig?
Is the food ready?

das Abendessen / Abendessen
dinner

Ich gehe heute zum Abendessen ins Restaurant.
I'm going to a restaurant for dinner tonight.

Culture note

You already know that there are two ways of addressing people. After you have known someone for a while, the person might suggest you use the informal du. Matthias suggests this to Lara in the video. To use the informal "you" is called duzen. To use the formal "you" is called siezen.

die Einladung / Einladungen
invitation

Vielen Dank für die Einladung.
Thank you for the invitation.

der Wein / Weine
wine

Trinkst du gerne Wein?
Do you like drinking wine?

das Huhn / Hühner
chicken

Ich esse gerne Huhn.
I like eating chicken.

kochen
to cook

Matthias kocht nicht gerne.
Matthias doesn't like cooking.

der Reis
rice

Heute gibt es Huhn mit Reis.
Today we have chicken with rice.

die Blume / Blumen
flower

Danke für die Blumen.
Thank you for the flowers.

lecker
tasty

Das Essen ist sehr lecker.
The food is really tasty.